Diesels in the Pennines

Derek Huntriss

First published 2002

ISBN 0 7110 2861 3

© Derek Huntriss 2002

Published by Ian Allan Publishing

an imprint of Ian Allan Publishing Ltd,
Hersham, Surrey KT12 4RG.
Printed by Ian Allan Printing Ltd,
Hersham, Surrey KT12 4RG.

Code: 0208/B2

Front Cover:
Dramatic evening lighting catches an unidentified English Electric Type 3 as it approaches Todmorden station in the Calder Valley at the head of a loaded westbound coal train on a June evening in 1970. *Robin Lush*

Rear Cover:
BR/Sulzer Type 2 No D5251 pilots Stanier Class 5 No 44667 up the 1 in 50 out of Bradford Exchange past St Dunstans Junction signalbox on 25 July 1967. *Peter Fitton*

This Page:
Photographed from the north end of the tunnel at Blea Moor, Brush/Sulzer Type 4 No 1941 catches the sun as it crosses Dent Head viaduct with an up fitted freight on 13 July 1971. *Peter Fitton*

Introduction

Upon nationalisation in 1948 the four big railway companies became British Railways and at that time there were 19,630 route miles in the railway system, BR employing some 641,046 people. Whilst electrification had been introduced in the south east and locally elsewhere, the steam locomotive reigned supreme with new types being designed and built.

However, within a few years drastic changes were to take place. In 1955, BR announced its Modernisation Plan with projected costs of £1,240 million to be spread over 15 years, a figure which in the event was greatly exceeded. A key aspect of this plan was the intention to abandon steam traction, the announcement coinciding with the continuing production of '9F' 2-10-0s.

Instead of introducing well proven designs of American construction, BR considered it to be politically preferable to place the Pilot Scheme orders with British manufacturers. This decision is now widely regarded as a serious misjudgment, incurring unnecessarily heavy costs for the British taxpayer. In 1956 the government decided to press ahead rapidly with dieselisation and between the years 1957 to 1968 over 16,000 steam locomotives were removed from service, some almost new, and were replaced by a variety of diesel locomotives. In some areas electrification was extended.

Maintenance of these early locomotives presented a major problem, most having to share outdated and unsuitable premises with steam. These problems were addressed by the construction of purpose-built diesel maintenance depots, the first of these being at Devons Road in north London. Most coaching stock was then not equipped for electric train heating, so many diesel locomotives were fitted with train heating boilers, which often took their weight over the specified axle loading and thus restricted their route availability.

With hindsight, BR would have benefited from the evolution of standard types from its pilot scheme designs. As it was, its policies resulted in a wide variety of non-standard types of varying quality, and much time, effort and money was wasted. However, to the enthusiast, the transition from steam was fascinating, with a number of diesel classes appearing and disappearing within a short span of years. Experiments with liveries, too, provided colourful contrasts with the grime and matt black of the ageing steam fleet.

Most railway photographers reserved their film for steam survivors, and colour photographs of early diesels are scarce. I am indebted to all those who contributed irreplaceable transparencies for inclusion in this book. We all owe them our sincere thanks for recording a period fast becoming as remote as the steam age itself. Stretching from Derby to Penrith and forming the backbone of England the Pennine region contains a vast spread of British Railways activity and has always presented a challenge to photographers eager to record the passing of both steam and diesel motive power. The glorious landscape of the region features strongly in this portrayal of the years of transition from steam to diesel motive power and is a showcase for modern traction photography.

This title takes the reader on a journey northwards from Derby criss-crossing the Pennines on many different routes and concluding with a journey from Settle to Carlisle.

Bibliography

Stephen R. Batty: *British Rail at Work: West Yorkshire;* Ian Allan
A.K. Butlin: *Diesel Disposal;* Coorlea Publishing
Ken Hoole: *Trains in Trouble - Vol. 3;* Atlantic Transport Publishers
Robert Stephens: *Diesel Pioneers;* Atlantic Transport Publishers
Alan R. Thompson & Ken Groundwater: *British Railways Past & Present No 11 North Yorkshire;* Silver Link Publishing

Also consulted: *British Rail Main Line Gradient Profiles;* Ian Allan
Magazines: *Backtrack; Modern Railways; Railway Magazine; Railway World; Traction; Trains Illustrated.*

Dedication

This title is dedicated to my close friend, the late Mick McNicholas of Hebden Bridge, whose burning enthusiasm for modern traction rekindled my interest in the subject.

Derek Huntriss
COVENTRY
June 2002

Newly constructed BR/Sulzer Type B No D5020 is portrayed outside the Diesel Test House at Derby Works in October 1959. Whilst undergoing testing, cables from the locomotive were connected to the test panel and resistances which were located in the upper storey of the Test House. The first five members of the class were powered by Sulzer engines built in Switzerland, other engines being built under licence by Vickers Armstrong of Barrow. The class was designed to a loading gauge of 12ft 8in, this allowing its use over the Widened Lines of the London Transport Executive. The first of the class, No D5000, entered revenue earning service on 15 September 1958 when it worked the 9.30am Derby to Manchester, 12.30pm Manchester to Liverpool Central, returning on the 2.30 pm Liverpool to Derby. *Raymond Reed*

Left: Production version, Brush Traction Co Type B No D5825, heads an up freight towards Derby ½ mile south of Duffield station on 30 April 1966. The first of the 20 pilot scheme locomotives, No D5500, was handed over to the BTC at a ceremony at the Brush locomotive works on 31 October 1957 and after trials between Loughborough and Chinley, made its first journey in revenue earning service with the 10.36am from Liverpool Street to Clacton on 13 November 1957. Prior to this working crew training had taken place between Shenfield and Southend (Victoria) and involved hauling 25 empty wagons between these points, the time allowed being 48 minutes. Similar workings with eight coaches were allowed 37 minutes.

Right: Also on 30 April 1966, BR/Sulzer Production 'Peak' 1Co-Co1 No D48 heads the northbound 'Devonian' near Duffield station. The 'Peaks' will always be associated with their duties on the Midland main line. The dieselisation of the Manchester services had been virtually completed by February 1961 and had led to a marked improvement in timekeeping. *Both: Mike Mensing*

Fresh from overhaul at Derby Works, BR/Sulzer Type 4 No D123 is seen near Duffield station on 30 April 1966 working the 14.00 Manchester (Central) to Nottingham (Midland). A new timetable had been introduced on 18 April, with only modest publicity; the procession of high-speed semi-fasts, local DMUs and long distance expresses all ran remarkably smoothly. *Mike Mensing*

The four-coach 17.26 from Sheffield to Derby is seen leaving Ambergate station behind 'Peak' No D47 in this panoramic view taken on 30 April 1966. With the introduction of the revised timetable on the Midland Lines several of the Manchester expresses were withdrawn including the runs made by the 'Midland Pullman'. An unfortunate disappearance was the 17.30 to Leeds which was replaced by two expresses to Sheffield. However, it was possible to leave Leeds for St Pancras 75 minutes later in the afternoon than hitherto. *Mike Mensing*

On Sunday 8 August 1965 'Peak' No D58 is depicted at the head of the 1.50pm St Pancras to Manchester as it approaches Cromford. At this time regular travellers may have been so used to seeing Type 4 2,500hp locomotives working trains on the Midland Lines that they may have forgotten that Metrovick-Crossley 1,200hp locomotives once hauled expresses between London and Manchester and the 'Condor' freight between Hendon and Gushetfaulds. Whilst mechanically they were not a success, with diagrammed mileages of over 500 achieved by them, they afforded a valuable background of experience with diesel traction before the advent of the Type 4s. For the planned elimination of steam working on the Midland Division, 122 Type 4 locomotives were authorised under the 1960 Building Programme. *Mike Mensing*

BR/Sulzer 'Peak' No D55 arrives at Matlock station with the 14.00 Manchester (Central) to St Pancras on Sunday 8 August 1965. Behind the train is a (4) x 2-car formation of 'Derby Lightweight' DMUs. The locomotive had been named *Royal Signals* five weeks earlier at a ceremony which took place on 30 June. Becoming Class 45 No 45144, it survived in traffic until 21 December 1987. *Mike Mensing*

Below: BR/Sulzer Bo-Bo No D5276 heads an empty train of ICI hoppers up the 1 in 90 climb out of Dove Holes tunnel in September 1967. The photographer well recalls his disappointment that the train was not steam hauled – time has since tempered his judgement. *Derek Huntriss*

Right: A sprinkling of light snow is on the ground in this 8 December 1967 view taken at Chinley station as No D54 *The Royal Pioneer Corps* leaves with a Manchester to Derby passenger working. Steam working in this area was to finish three months later on 4 March 1968. *Les Nixon*

Left: Displaced from its traditional duties by the introduction of Inter-City 125 units in 1983, Class 45 No 45037 is seen with a more mundane duty as it heads an empty Peak stone train towards Chinley North Junction on 22 February 1986. No 45037 was to continue in traffic for another two years until a generator flashover gave cause for its withdrawal on 27 July 1988. However it wasn't until 13 November 1992 that it was cut up at MC Metals of Springburn in Glasgow.

Above: Snow is still falling in this view of snow-covered Class 20s Nos 20034 and 20160 as they wait for their next turn of snowplough duty at Buxton depot on 8 February 1986. To highlight the importance of these duties it is interesting to note that during 1983 some 90,000 wagon loads were moved out of the Buxton area, recording an enormous 3.3million tonnes of bulk ore carried on BR, a triumph for rail supremacy over road with both social and environmental benefits, not to mention revenue. *Both: Hugh Ballantyne*

Left: BR/Sulzer Class 25 No 25281 catches the sunlight as it heads a train of loaded ICI wagons round the curve at Buxworth with a Tunstead to Northwich train on 15 July 1978. This working runs almost daily excepting the Christmas period, the Class 25s having taken over from Stanier '8F's in March 1968. Other classes used on these duties have included pairs of Class 37s or 20s, Classes 40 and 47 with occasional use of Class 31s. This section of the former Midland Railway was widened to accommodate four tracks in 1902 and the tunnel which had previously existed at Buxworth was demolished and replaced with a deep cutting. Present day improvements in motive power and reductions in traffic have once again seen a return to a straightforward double track layout, the two lines farthest from the camera having been removed. *Les Nixon*

Right: Once again in Buxworth cutting, this time on 22 February 1986, English Electric Class 20s Nos 20183 and 20148 are seen at the head of an empty ICI hopper train. With a service availability approaching 90%, the Class 20s had the acclaim of their drivers and maintenance men, no fewer than 176 still being in use at May 1988. *Hugh Ballantyne*

Left: Class 40 No 40115 makes her way sedately down Edale, near Edale Station, with a block empty cement train for Earle's Sidings, Hope, on 18 October 1980. The Class 40 locomotives were built at the Vulcan (Newton-le-Willows) works of English Electric, with the exceptions of Nos D305-24 which came from the Darlington Robert Stephenson & Hawthorn works, by that time, of course, also part of English Electric.

Above: Class 25 No 25308 is seen in deep snow at Earle's Sidings in the Hope Valley on 27 January 1979. The limited siding facilities at Earle's, introduced when the nearby cement works opened in 1930, have for many years been barely sufficient to handle the growing cement and coal traffic. Today most of the shunting movements are handled by a resident Andrew Barclay Bo-Bo, specifically built for the job, previously contracted to a Class 08 from Tinsley.
Both: Les Nixon

17

Above: Hoar frost clings to the bushes and telegraph wires as Class 47 No 47473 shunts an engineers' train at Bamford on 1 December 1978. As part of track rationalisation both the down siding and the up loop have been eliminated here–along with the goods shed. The signalbox has been removed and relocated to Peak Rail at Darley Dale.

Right: Class 25 No 25168 is seen at Hathersage with a Balne Lane to Peak Forest empties. Of 477 BR/Sulzer Type 2s constructed, the first 151 members were designated as Class 24, the remainder, having an uprated 1,250hp Sulzer engine and redesigned body, becoming Class 25s, the final members being withdrawn in 1987. *Both: Les Nixon*

When the direct route from Manchester to St Pancras via Peak Forest closed in 1968, a remnant of a through service ran via the Hope Valley, but on Sundays only. Here BR/Sulzer 'Peak' No D39 rounds the curve at Grindleford on 20 April 1969. No D39, later became Class 45 No 45133 under TOPS, and was to remain in traffic for almost a further 20 years, until, as a result of a generator flashover, it was withdrawn on 4 February 1988. The locomotive had received its last overhaul at Crewe Locomotive Works on 27 September 1983 and it wasn't until 10 February 1992 that it was broken up at MC Metals at Springburn in Glasgow. *Les Nixon*

Clayton Equipment Co Bo-Bo Type 1 No D8613 is seen at Glapwell Colliery on 16 October 1965. It had been attached to the rear of the RCTS 'Midland Locomotive Requiem' railtour at Seymour Junction and had acted as pilot to Midland '4F' No 43953, the last Midland-designed tender engine, over the adverse gradients to the colliery sidings. No D8613 had been put into traffic at Tinsley in the period to 6 February 1965 together with sister loco No D8612. Other new diesels placed into traffic at Tinsley at that date were Nos D1792, D1798-D1803, D1805, D1806 and D6959-D6965. By the end of 1968 no members of the class remained in service on the London Midland Region; those that had not been withdrawn or stored unserviceable, were transferred to the Scottish Region. However, it was not until August 1975 that No D8613 was sold for disposal to McWilliams at Shettleston. *Neville Simms*

21

Left: Class 31 No 31204 and Class 37 No 37169 double-head a Wath to Earle's Sidings coal train through Millhouses. Much has changed since this picture was taken on 21 July 1982. The four-track main line has been reduced to two, the remains of Millhouses station have been demolished and the yard at Wath completely obliterated. *Les Nixon*

Below: Green-liveried Type 4 No 1988 awaits departure with an up express from Platform 5 at Sheffield Midland on 10 November 1971. Initially, the first batch of the class proved to be no more reliable than any other diesel class, but after eliminating teething troubles they were to give sterling service for many years. *Andrew Wiltshire*

Above: Class 25s Nos D7595 and D7597 pass Torside level crossing on the Woodhead route with one of six football excursions taking Manchester United supporters to Wadsley Bridge to see the semi-final of the FA cup against Leeds United at Hillsborough on 14 March 1970. Motive power on the other specials included three green Class 40s, a blue 'Peak' and Class 50 No D414. *Gavin Morrison*

Right: Taken on the same day as the previous picture, another 'Footex' special over Woodhead produced what was believed to be the only known working of a Class 50 over the route. This striking picture features No D414 rounding the curve at Torside at the head of the special. With the energising of the West Coast main line in spring 1974 the class was eventually transferred to the Western Region. *Robin Lush*

English Electric Class 40 No 40155 (formerly D355) is seen under the wires at Guide Bridge on 31 July 1984. Delivery of the first production batch of the class began in May 1959, after which a further six batches were constructed, bringing the total number of the class in traffic to 200. The first of the production batch, No D211, also had the distinction of being the first member of the class to arrive in Glasgow Central when it worked the 4.15pm from Crewe to Glasgow on 19 August 1960. The class was to become one of the most successful of the pilot scheme types, some examples soldiering on in traffic for over 25 years. *Andrew Wiltshire*

Brush/Sulzer Type 4 No 1834 awaits departure from Manchester Piccadilly on 27th May 1972 with the 'Boat Train' for Harwich Parkeston Quay. This train, which ran via the Hope Valley, had been transferred when regular passenger traffic over its former route, Woodhead, finished the previous year. Smart running was required with only 40 minutes turn round time at Manchester. *Les Nixon*

Left: In a typical Pennine setting with steep hills, mill chimneys, chapels and canal, 'Deltic' Class 55 No 55017 *The Durham Light Infantry* catches the late evening light as it crosses Saddleworth viaduct with the 17.05 Liverpool to Newcastle on 23 July 1979. Having been displaced from their East Coast main line duties, some members of the class were given an extended lease of life on Trans-Pennine services, duties which continued until 27 December 1981. *Robin Lush*

Above: Another late evening picture taken at Saddleworth viaduct depicts this time Class 45 No 45138 with a westbound working, the 15.57 Scarborough to Liverpool, on 7 July 1984. Just over two years later, on 22 December 1986, No 45138 was withdrawn from traffic after suffering a fire, its final working being the 1E78 Birmingham to Leeds on 1 December. However, as with other members of the class, it was not until 1994 that it was finally scrapped. *Hugh Ballantyne*

Above: Work-stained Class 47 No 47480 climbs the last mile of the 1 in 125 ascent past Diggle to Standedge tunnel with the 08.10 from Liverpool to Newcastle through a snow-covered Pennine landscape on 24 February 1979. *John Whiteley*

30

Right: After passing through Standedge tunnel, green-liveried Brush/Sulzer Type 4 No 1839 drifts down the 1 in 105 from Marsden to Huddersfield near Longwood Goods with a Liverpool to Newcastle express on 15 April 1974. *David C. Rodgers*

BR/Sulzer 'Peak' Type 4 No D177 (later Class 46 No 46040) passes through Paddock cutting, west of Huddersfield, on the morning Newcastle express on 20 August 1966. Construction of the 56 locomotives in the class was carried out at BR's Derby Locomotive works, deliveries being made between October 1961 and January 1963. At first the class was divided between the then North Eastern Region, and the London Midland Region based at Derby. In preparation for their introduction on inter-regional services, depot familiarisation saw allocations to the Western Region and in Scotland, as well as on the Eastern Region and elsewhere on the LMR. Gateshead was also very quick to employ Class 46s on the Newcastle to Liverpool trains. No 46040 was to survive in traffic until December 1980. *Gavin Morrison*

Taken some 13 years later at the same location as the previous picture, Class 47 No 47429 approaches Huddersfield at Paddock with the 08.10 from Liverpool to Newcastle on 24 February 1979. It can easily be seen that the four-track formation at this point has been reduced to two in the intervening years, the two tracks nearest the camera having been removed. *John Whiteley*

Left: 'Deltic' No 55015 *Tulyar*, suitably adorned with a rosette, stands in Huddersfield station as it heads the last 'Deltic'-hauled Liverpool to York express on 27th December 1981.

Above: Class 37 No 37067 crosses Lockwood viaduct on the Penistone to Huddersfield line with coal empties for Clayton West on 4 September 1980. *Both: David C. Rodgers*

Above: Total glitter as the photographer catches Class 47 No 47542 erupting from the fly-under at Heaton Lodge Junction with the 17.05 Liverpool to Newcastle on 26 June 1979. In 1970 the Heaton Lodge area was relaid, with the flat junction between the Calder Valley and Huddersfield routes converted into a burrowing junction. *Robin Lush*

Right: Still in green livery but carrying its new TOPS number which it received in February 1974, English Type 4 No 40169 (D369) heads an up mixed freight past the former Mirfield MPD on 29 May 1974. The new Healey Mills diesel depot which opened in 1966 had rendered Mirfield shed redundant and it closed on 2 January 1967. *Gavin Morrison*

Diverted from the Standedge route for engineering work to be carried out, Class 47 No 47401 heads towards the tunnel at Sowerby Bridge on the Calder Valley route with the 09.55 Newcastle to Liverpool on Sunday 16 September 1979. The site of the former steam depot at Sowerby Bridge can be seen behind the train. Compared to the Standedge route this line provides an easier run for MGR and tank trains, the bulk of the latter consisting of oil trains from Preston, Manchester and Stanlow with return workings from Newcastle, Immingham or Leeds. Whilst the line could not be described as heavily used, in 1979 it was considered a marginal case for closure. *J. Whiteley*

This view, also taken during Sunday diversions over the Calder Valley route on 16 September 1979, depicts Class 46 No 46046 after crossing Horsfall viaduct, between Todmorden and Hebden Bridge, with the 08.40 from Liverpool to Newcastle. No 46046 was to survive until 6 May 1984 when it was withdrawn due to bogie fractures, scrapping taking place at Doncaster Works. *John Whiteley*

Below: A further view showing Calder Valley diversions on Sunday 16 September 1979, this time depicting an unidentified Class 25 as it crosses Horsfall viaduct with the Hull to Manchester (Red Bank) empty van train. *John Whiteley*

Right: Pennine cottages dot the hillside and dramatic evening lighting catches the telegraph wires as English Electric Type 3 No 6927 crosses Gauxholme viaduct, south of Todmorden, with a loaded westbound coal train consisting of standard 16-ton mineral wagons. *Robin Lush*

Left: A more detailed view is shown of the original 1840 turreted viaduct over the Rochdale Canal at Gauxholme as Class 47 No 47088 *SAMSON* heads the diverted 12.20 Newcastle to Liverpool on Sunday 23 September 1979. Regular passenger trains over this route at that time were mainly in the capable hands of the Rolls-Royce-powered Class 110 DMUs. These had replaced steam services in 1960/1 and were still doing the job for which they had been designed. *John Whiteley*

Above: Only weeks away from withdrawal 'Peak' Class 45 No 45102 descends from Summit Tunnel with the Newcastle to Manchester (Red Bank) vans in August 1986. Summit Tunnel came very close to permanent closure on 20 December 1984 when a loaded petrol tank train was derailed inside it and caught fire. The fire raged for four days, with flames shooting out of the ventilation shafts. After damage to a short section was repaired, it reopened on 9 August 1985. *D. Huntriss*

An unidentified green-liveried Class 47 enters Holme tunnel on the climb to the 749ft Copy Pit summit, between Burnley and Todmorden, with what was believed to be a football excursion returning to the London area on 29 August 1970.

The Beeching Report concluded that Copy Pit was ripe for development, particularly for freight haulage, and in due course Preston power signalbox extended its area of control over the route and along the Calder Valley to Hebden Bridge. With the Todmorden to Rose Grove (Burnley) passenger service having disappeared in 1965 only a daily Leeds-Blackpool service and several 'Wakes Weeks' holiday trains were left as the regular passenger workings.

Until the late 1970s the freight flowed in considerable quantity but the recession of the early 1980s bit hard and freight traffic was in decline.

In 1984 BR was planning to introduce five trains a day from Leeds to Preston when fate took a hand. The National Provincial Building Society moved a large part of its office accommodation from the Burnley area to Bradford, so in order to avoid staff having to face a difficult journey to work, it was agreed to run a service of trains from Preston, these eventually being supplemented by the five trains from Leeds.
Robin Lush

The twin cooling towers of Huncoat power station dominate the skyline in this view of a green-liveried Class 40 approaching Rose Grove, Burnley, with a freight for Healey Mills on 10 June 1968. The photographer well recalls his disappointment as this should have been a steam-hauled working. The steam depot at Rose Grove closed on 4 August 1968, the diesels taking over the last remaining duties which included a frequent service of coal trains between Burnley and Burn Naze in addition to through freight traffic from Preston to Healey Mills over Copy Pit. These and some express freight workings had kept about 25 Stanier Class 8Fs and a handful of Class 5s fairly busy. *Robin Lush*

In this panoramic view of Accrington taken on 28 August 1970, preserved green-liveried Stanier Class 5 No 44806 is being piloted by a Class 25 for its journey to an open day at Helmshore on the embryonic East Lancs Railway via Copy Pit, Rochdale and Heywood. No 44806 had arrived at Accrington on 6 April 1970 in the 16.26 Heysham to Healey Mills freight which was hauled by Class 40 No 394. The steam locomotive had been 'tripped' from Carnforth before its move to Accrington for storage in the diesel multiple-unit depot which can be seen in the background. *Robin Lush*

On the former Lancashire & Yorkshire Railway route from Whalley to Blackburn attractive two-tone green liveried BR/Sulzer Type 2 No D5255 (later Class 25 No 25105) heads a freight from Carlisle near Wilpshire on 20 April 1968. Withdrawn from Longsight diesel depot in April 1982, No 25105 met the cutter`s torch at the former Great Western locomotive works at Swindon in November 1985. *Peter Fitton*

With the Pennine hills beyond Lancaster as a backdrop, Metropolitan-Vickers 1,200hp Co-Bo Type 2 No D5707 approaches Morecambe Promenade with the fully-fitted 18.50 Heysham Moss to Whitehaven tank train on 6 July 1964. New Year's Day, 1966, saw the last regular passenger services over the 14-mile Wennington-Lancaster-Morecambe section of the former Midland Railway, while the $4^1/_2$-mile line to Heysham remained open for boat-train traffic. The Lancaster, Morecambe and Heysham 6.6kV electric line, opened in 1908, was, in 1953, to give useful technical data for the adoption of 25kV electrification between Euston and Glasgow. *Derrick Codling*

With end of steam traction on BR rapidly approaching, BR/Sulzer Type 2 No D5181 pilots Class 9F 2-10-0 No 92167 at Wennington on 29 May 1968 with 4N28, the 12.06 Heysham to Haverton Hill tank train.

At that time it was still possible for this working to be hauled by two steam locomotives, one being from Holbeck (55A) MPD. No D5181 became No 25031 and was scrapped at Glasgow Works in 1978. *Peter Fitton*

49

Left: Photographed at Clapham, junction for the line to Low Gill, BR/Sulzer Type 2 No D7592 (renumbered Class 25 No 25242 in February 1974) is at the head of a Morecambe to Leeds train on 12 March 1966. Services such as this, consisting of seven corridor coaches, have now been replaced by two-coach 'Pacers' and Class 156 diesel multiple-units. *Gavin Morrison*

Above: An unidentified EE Type 4 is seen leaving Hellifield station heading north on 7 February 1970. Without doubt the single most publicised event to befall any diesel locomotive happened to an EE Type 4 on 8 August 1963. No D326 was hauling the 6.50pm Glasgow to Euston mail when it was halted by a masked gang at Sears Crossing who proceeded to rob the train of an estimated £2,500,000. *Robin Lush*

English Electric 2,700hp Type 4 No 50035 leaves Hellifield with a southbound freight on 8 March 1975. The class, known as 'Warships' following their allocation to the Western Region, were later nicknamed 'Hoovers' by enthusiasts. Their history derives from the inadequacy of the Type 4 classes available to the London Midland Region in the mid-1960s to provide the fast timings required on the West Coast main line beyond the northern limit of electric traction at Crewe, their general specification evolving from the prototype DP2. Designed as high-speed units they shared the distinction with the 'Deltics' of being the only diesel classes to run up to 100mph. *David Rodgers*

Freshly outshopped in BR corporate blue livery, Class 45 No D20 is seen leaving Hellifield with an eastbound freight on 15 June 1968. Always synonymous with the lines of the former Midland Railway, there were sufficient members of Class 45 to allow the introduction of an accelerated timetable in September 1962, although these were handicapped by a severe winter. *Robin Lush*

An unidentified English Electric Type 4 approaches Gargrave with a down freight on 27 December 1968. The original 10 members of the class (D200-D209), were to be classed as Type C, having an engine rated at 2,000bhp, but when the power classification system was changed they fell into the Type 4 category for units of over 2,000hp, but under 3,000hp. Five subsequent orders increased the class to 200, the final delivery being made in September 1962. The design was the product of the English Electric Company and had certain features in common with the Southern Railway's prototype diesels 10201-3. The 16-cylinder diesel engine was first used in this country in the LMS prototypes Nos 10000/1, and with further development, has been used in Class 50 and 56 diesels, its power output being doubled. *John Whiteley*

Sheep dot the landscape in this bucolic view taken on 27 June 1979 as Class 25 No 25282 heads an Inspection Saloon along the freight-only branch to Swinden Quarry at Rylstone on the southern fringe of the Yorkshire Dales, seven miles north of Skipton and three miles from the picturesque Wharfedale village of Grassington. Passenger services on the line were withdrawn in 1930. *Robin Lush*

The golden hue of late evening light glitters along the sides of a pair of Class 25s in this stunning picture taken at Skipton on 6 June 1970. The train is the southbound car train from Linwood in Scotland to Gosford Green in Coventry and carries brand-new Hillman Imps which are heading south for distribution. The Hillman Imps were the only cars to be built in Scotland and why there are some Hillman Hunters in the consist is something of a mystery. For the record the freight-only branch from Three Spires Junction to Gosford Green in Coventry is now part of an Orbital Relief Road and provides a speedy transit from the north to the south of the city. *Robin Lush*

Semaphores abound in this view taken at Skipton on 31 May 1968 as a green Class 47 leaves with an eastbound freight. In the background a BR Standard Class 4 will marshal a train for the Grassington branch. At that time, one or two short loose-coupled freight trains a day traversed the branch; this was about to change as fast high-capacity rail loading facilities were installed at the quarry between 1970 and 1973. *R. Lush*

This picture, taken west of Keighley on 20 June 1962, depicts English Electric Type 4 No D242 heading towards Leeds at the head of a rake of former LNER stock. This train which at that time ran every weekday between Leeds and Appleby was to train drivers in the use of diesel traction. Normally a Class 40 was used for this exercise although Class 37s were observed on occasions. No D242 came to be renumbered 40042 under TOPS in February 1974 and was withdrawn from Longsight depot in December 1980. *Gavin Morrison*

Two-tone green liveried BR/Sulzer Type 2 No D5252 was photographed heading west near Shipley with a special inter-regional working on 20 August 1966. The new BR Type 2s, later Class 25s, were in production between 1961 and 1967. During this period, advances in technology brought alterations to the design of the electrical equipment and control gear, giving rise to the sub-classes 25/0-25/3. *Peter Fitton*

Left: A classic view of the down 'Thames-Clyde Express' as it heads north past Shipley behind an unidentified 'Peak' on 16 November 1974. On the withdrawal of all main-line and most local services from Bradford Forster Square, Shipley would have been without a Leeds service had the Leeds-Skipton trains not begun to reverse into the station. It was not until May 1979 that a single platform was opened on the Leeds-Keighley curve and May 1981 that Keighley-Leeds trains could access this platform. *John S. Whiteley*

Above: Prototype English Electric 2,700hp Co-Co No DP2 waits for departure from Bradford Exchange with the up 'Yorkshire Pullman' on 18 February 1967. Having become derailed, but not damaged, at Edinburgh Waverley in August 1966, it was only five months after this picture was taken, on 31 July 1967, whilst working the 12.00 Kings Cross to Edinburgh, that No DP2 struck some derailed cement wagons at Thirsk. Unfortunately seven passengers were killed and 45 injured in this tragic accident; No DP2 was beyond economic repair. *Peter J. Fitton*   61

Above: Two-tone green-liveried Brush Type 4 No 1109 leaves Bradford Interchange with a London train on 15 June 1973. Initially, the first batch of Brush Type 4s had been no more reliable than any other diesel class and from 25 October 1963, Nos D1546/7 from the next batch were worked continuously on six Finsbury Park diagrams until they failed, the object being to gauge and then eliminate the teething problems which had plagued the early batch. With many detail differences between class members, the survivors now approach the end of their lives. *R. Lush*

Right: A classic action shot of the transition from steam to diesel traction as green-liveried EE Type 4 No D348 (later 40148) climbs the 1 in 50 out of Bradford Exchange on 9 June 1967. This was one of three special workings taking Grattan Warehouses employees to Blackpool, excursions which in previous years had been in the hands of steam traction. Class 40 No 40148 was withdrawn from traffic at Longsight depot in August 1982 and was stored at Stratford until February 1983. *Peter J. Fitton*

Left: Class 24 No D5100 pilots an unidentified Fairburn 2-6-4T with a King's Cross working out of Bradford Exchange past St Dunstans Junction in June 1967. The Class 24s were constructed at three BR workshops, Derby, Crewe and Darlington. Nos D5000-29, 5066-75 and 5114-50 were built at Derby, D5030-65/76-93 at Crewe, with D5100 being part of the batch D5094-D5113 constructed at Darlington. The first member of the class to be withdrawn was as early as November 1967 when No D5051 was taken out of service, reportedly after fire damage. *John S. Whiteley*

Right: This view, taken at Stanningley on 3 July 1967, also depicts a Class 24 piloting a steam loco with a King's Cross express. Class 24 No D5098 pilots Low Moor (56F) MPD's Stanier Class 5 No 44912 with a full train which required two locomotivess, other workings from Bradford Exchange to King's Cross being only portions. In an adjacent siding one of the last surviving Thompson Class B1 4-6-0s, No 61306, is with a train from which bricks are being unloaded. No 61306 was to have the honour of hauling the last steam-hauled 'Yorkshire Pullman' between Bradford and Leeds on 30 September 1967. *Peter J. Fitton*

Horbury & Ossett station is in the background of this picture showing grimy Class 37 No D6867 with an eastbound freight on 18 March 1967. Six hundred yards west of Horbury & Ossett station box and that station's island platform is Healey Mills East box, controlling the outlet from Healey Mills marshalling yard, which lies on the down (northern) side of the four tracks.

At the other end of the yard and 1,358 yards away is Healey Mills West box. Healey Mills was a natural concentration point for east-west flows of freight. On one side it had convenient rail links with the industrial West Riding and North East and the ports of Hull and Goole, and on the other with industrial Lancashire and the Merseyside ports. *J. N. Simms*

Looking strangely out of place in this predominantly steam environment, 'Deltic' Class 55 No D9001 *St Paddy* heads the three-coach 2.05pm Leeds Central to Doncaster stopping train past the former Lancashire & Yorkshire steam sheds at Wakefield on 7 September 1961. In the background are stored two former L&Y Aspinall 0-6-0s. At that time this train was being used to train drivers in the use of the new diesel locomotives. A revolutionary series of accelerations was planned for the 1961 summer timetable, but in the event the 'Deltics' were not ready and the recast timetable was postponed for a year, the non-stop 'Elizabethan' had just one last unexpected summer with Class A4 haulage. In the winter 1961/62 timetable certain trains diagrammed for 'Deltics' were accelerated: prime example was the 7.45am Kings Cross to Leeds between Hitchin and Retford, the start to stop schedule for the 106.9 miles being at an average of 71.9mph. *Gavin Morrison*

Above: This view, taken on 29 April 1967, sees Class 47/4 No D1103 (later No 47520) heading the up 'Yorkshire Pullman' past the site of the former steam MPD at Copley Hill as the train approaches Wortley Junction, south of Leeds. In the background are the carriage sheds which continued in use until the closure of Leeds Central on 1 May 1967, two days after this picture was taken. *Gavin Morrison*

Right: Weeks before the closure of Leeds Central on 18 February 1967, English Electric prototype Co-Co No DP2 prepares to leave for Bradford with the 'Yorkshire Pullman' from Kings Cross. No DP2 had been transferred from the LMR to the Eastern Region at the manufacturer's request in mid-July 1963, its first duties being the 12.45pm Kings Cross to Leeds and 3pm back on 13 July. *P.J. Fitton*

BR/Sulzer production series 'Peak' No D174 (later Class 46 No 46037) passes the closed station at Arthington, near Leeds, with the 15.16 Newcastle to Liverpool (Lime Street) on 17 July 1965. Arthington, just north of Bramhope tunnel on the line from Leeds to Harrogate, had two stations, the first which was opened in 1849. It was moved to another site in 1865 due to its original position becoming somewhat inconvenient as a junction station for the branch to Ilkley and the west. Permanent facilities were added in 1876 before rebuilding which followed in 1896. The overall result, seen in this view, was the somewhat shabby-looking building, which had closed in March 1965. *Mike Mensing*

This fascinating view of central Leeds, taken on 18 April 1967 from the closed station at Holbeck High Level, shows Class 25 No D5177 (later No 25027) turning at Gelderd Junction on to the lines for Leeds Central with the 'Yorkshire Pullman' from Harrogate to King's Cross. Major changes to Pullman timings came in May 1971 when greatly-accelerated 'Deltic' turns were introduced. The load was then eight cars throughout from Harrogate, leaving at 09.48. After calling at Leeds City, Wakefield was left at 10.43 and a non-stop run over the 178.5 miles to King's Cross brought the train into London at 13.16. No 25027 was to survive in traffic until May 1983. *Peter J. Fitton*

Below: Green-liveried 'Peak' Class 45/0 No D76 (later No 45053) comes off the Settle and Carlisle route at Settle Junction with an up freight on 12 March 1966. No 45053 was withdrawn in November 1983 and scrapped at Crewe Works in October 1988.

Right: On a glorious sunny day two-tone green-liveried Class 47 No D1545 (later No 47431) has the easy task of hauling a local pick-up freight to Carlisle past Horton-in-Ribblesdale on 29 November 1969. *Both: Gavin Morrison*

Left: Class 47 No D1852 (later 47202) and Class 25 No D7543 (later 25193) double-head an up Settle & Carlisle freight past the closed signalbox at Dent Head on 17 July 1971. After passing the box at Dent Head the line crosses Dent Dale on a 10-span viaduct before plunging 500ft below the surface of the moor into the 2,629yd-long Blea Moor Tunnel. Alongside the wind-battered signalbox at Blea Moor a milepost indicates a distance of 248^1/$_2$ miles from St Pancras. *P. J. Fitton*

Above: Class 50 No 50021 crosses Dandry Mire viaduct with the 09.57 Carlisle to Euston on Sunday 16 March 1975. Sunday diversions caused by engineering work on the West Coast main line found the class tackling the grades to Ais Gill on the Settle & Carlisle line, as well as skirting the east side of Manchester on the way between Preston and Crewe via Stockport. The last four members of the class left Crewe Diesel Depot for the WR in May 1976. *David C. Rodgers*

Above: The snow is lying at Blea Moor as Class 40 No D268 passes with the up milk train from Appleby on 14 February 1970. A year earlier the closure of the 'Waverley' route had deprived the Settle & Carlisle of one of its expresses. In 1970 only two daytime passenger trains remained. The 'Thames-Clyde' still journeyed from St Pancras to Glasgow and there was a morning train from Leeds to Glasgow returning in the evening. It wasn't even possible to get from Carlisle to Leeds and back in the same day. *Gavin Morrison*

Right: Superb late-afternoon lighting conditions colour the stunning landscape as triple-headed super power takes the 12.42 Carlisle to Leeds service across Lunds Viaduct, north of Garsdale, on Saturday 25 November 1989. Class 20 Nos 20093 and 20061 assist Class 47 No 47444 with the 12-coach load, the Class 47 being provided for train heating purposes. The success of the 1,000hp Bo-Bo Class 20s lay with the design, which incorporated well-proven equipment. *Hugh Ballantyne*

Above: An unidentified BR Corporate-blue-liveried 'Peak' Class 45 heads a northbound Settle & Carlisle passenger working through a snow-covered landscape over Lunds Viaduct on 14 February 1970. In 1975 S&C passenger services were supplemented by the introduction of 'Dales Rail'. On one weekend a month, nine disused stations came back to life, DMUs bringing visitors into the Dales. *Robin Lush*

Right: In 1978, BR, most commendably reinstated Class 40 No 40122 to traffic and repainted it in original livery with BR totems, but with yellow nose-ends. It is seen here approaching Ais Gill on 16 September 1984 with the 16.00 Leeds to Carlisle service. After withdrawal, this celebrity machine was bought by Gerald Boden and subsequently named *Atlantic Conveyor. Derek Huntriss*

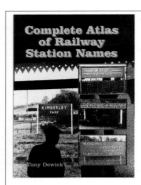
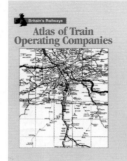

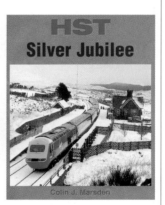